The Seal of Faith

A True Story as told by Joanasie Benjamin Arreak
to George Otis, Jr. and Paul Scotchmer

Illustrations by
Pete Berg

This happened a long time ago. It is not written. My grandfather told me under the stars. His name was Angutirjuaq [Angwa-ti-zowach].

We lived on the northern shore of the big island — the one the Anglos call Baffin.

Angutirjuaq was the spiritual leader of our clan. He helped our people, the Inuit, form their thoughts. He told us when it was time to break camp and move on.

When Angutirjuaq was getting to have hair like snow, he heard about God from an Inuk who had come up from the South.

The Inuk spoke of a new belief, of someone named Jesusie. He said He was the Son of God.

At first Angutirjuaq did not understand what he heard, but he was curious, for his job was to explain spiritual mysteries to the people.

And that is when the hidden things began to move inside himself.

A vision came to him: he went on a long journey to search for the truth.

For a long time he could find nothing.

But one day he found a place where the light and dark came together. He could not go into the light or into the dark, so he climbed into a gap between them.

He went up and up and up, until he found a door. But he could not get in. And so he awoke from his dream.

Angutirjuaq could not understand this. He thought maybe the door would open if he followed after the Inuk's God.

A desire was burning inside him…and so he decided to give himself to this new faith.

There is an Inuit way. When the people want to give their whole heart to something, they make a ritual. So Angutirjuaq thought he would kill a seal so that the people might share its meat and blood together.

That is when he told his people, "I'm going to hunt seal. If I catch one tonight, it will be a sign. I will give my life to the Inuk's God, and practice this ritual. But if I don't catch anything, I'm not going to do it."

It was the season of snow. The sky was very dark. There was no moon and no stars that night. Just heavy clouds.

Angutirjuaq knew it would be hard to find a seal.

But he wanted to do it. So he went out on the frozen ocean to look for a breathing hole.

Even in the dark he found one. But the seal was not there. He had to wait.

It was very cold, so he built a little wall of ice to protect himself from the wind. Then he sat down and made his harpoon ready to strike the seal.

When after some time the seal didn't come, he fell asleep.

While Angutirjuaq was sleeping the dream came again. He saw it until his head fell and he woke up.

When he opened his eyes he looked down at the breathing hole. There was something different, but at first he didn't understand what it was.

Then he realized he could see his shadow—something very strange on a moonless, winter night.

…and that was when he saw them.

Angutirjuaq saw three beings that looked like they had wings.

Wings!

They were coming down from out of the clouds, and light was falling off them.

They did not speak, but Angutirjuaq knew why they had come.

As soon as they left, a seal came out of the hole.

Angutirjuaq put the harpoon into it and dragged it back to camp.

The people were still sleeping.

Later they came out of their igloos and shared that seal.

That is when Angutirjuaq and his people started to follow Jesusie.

Many years later, the missionaries came and told us the whole story about God and His Son, as it is written in the Great Book.

And we knew it was so.

Joanasie Benjamin Arreak

More than 100 years ago, Joanasie [Ju-ońe-na-see] Benjamin Arreak's grandfather, Angutirjuaq, heard stories about a life-changing God. These accounts were brought to him by an Inuk from beyond Baffin Island. Angutirjuaq was a spiritual leader for his people, the Inuit, and was responsible for explaining spiritual truths.

In *The Seal of Faith*, Joanasie Benjamin recounts the story — to his son James *and to us* — of how the Gospel reached the Inuit of Baffin Island.

James Arreak and his father, Joanasie Benjamin Arreak

God Speaks Through Symbols, Visions and Dreams

Holy Communion God has inspired many cultural customs according to His ways. The tradition of eating a kill was common practice for the Inuit. The reason for eating together signified a moment in time where an important decision was made. Angutirjuaq shared the seal with the community to let everyone know of his decision to follow this new God. Eating the seal was symbolic of this decision. Later, it was through the Bible that they learned of the body and blood of Christ.

Visions and Dreams God has given people dreams and visions since Biblical times. Jacob's dream about the ladder to heaven, Joseph's dream about Mary becoming his wife and Paul's powerful vision of Christ on the Road to Damascus are a few of the many examples in the Bible. Angutirjuaq, like these people, had a vision. He felt this vision was from God and meant something to him. It not only changed his life but also the lives of his descendents.

Glossary of Terms

Baffin Island — A large island in the Eastern Canadian Arctic in the Region of Nunavut

Anglo — A term used referring to the white man

Aboriginal — The first people living on the land

Inuit — The aboriginal people who live on Baffin Island — it is plural, meaning more than one Inuk

Inuk — The Inuit word for one Inuit person

Jesusie — [Gee-sóo-see] A name used by the Inuit for Jesus Christ

Igloo — Homes built of large blocks of ice

The Great Book — A term used by the Inuit for the Holy Bible

Learn more about…

Angutirjuaq and his descendents in the award-winning video, *Transformations* II: *The Glory Spreads*. This video not only tells the story of when missionaries first came to the Canadian Arctic but also how Christianity has changed the way people live there today.

For more stories about how God is changing families, neighborhoods and cities around the world, watch the first *Transformations* video.

You can order these videos from:

TransformNations Media

P.O. Box 6334, Lynnwood, WA 98036 USA

from our Website: www.TransformNations.com

or by calling 1(800) 668-5657